Original title:
The Joy of Sunlight on My Skin

Copyright © 2025 Creative Arts Management OÜ
All rights reserved.

Author: George Mercer
ISBN HARDBACK: 978-3-69081-216-0
ISBN PAPERBACK: 978-3-69081-712-7

Light's Gentle Embrace

A solar hug upon my cheek,
I laugh as shadows dance and sneak.
The sun's warm glare like silly beams,
Chasing away my sleepy dreams.

The grass tickles my toes so free,
I giggle as I spot a bee.
It buzzes by with such delight,
As I bask in this glowing light.

Euphoria in Every Gleam

Oh what a sight, the sun's bright glint,
My glasses slide off, and I squint.
With rays that tickle and tease my skin,
I grin wide as the warmth creeps in.

A squirrel joins in with a jump and twist,
I wonder if it's sunlight's gift.
It's laughing too, in its furry way,
Perhaps we'll dance till the end of day.

Days Bathed in Radiance

I forget to fret, it's time to play,
The sun spills joy in endless array.
Splashing in puddles left by the dawn,
With every gleam, my worries are gone.

Chocolate ice cream melts in the heat,
It drips on my shirt—oh, what a treat!
Sticky fingers and giggles take flight,
This radiant day feels just so right.

The Play of Shadows

Shapes on the ground start to prance,
As sunlight leads a silly dance.
With every twist and every turn,
The shadows laugh, and I discern.

A dance-off here with playful light,
I lose my shadow, what a sight!
As I twirl, the sun beams wide,
In this funny game, I take great pride.

Sunlit Dreams

Beams of warmth dance on my nose,
Like a puppy that joyfully chose.
Tickling toes with sunlit flair,
I giggle while I lose my hair.

Spinning in circles like a whirlybird,
Sun-kissed skin, oh how absurd!
I swear I'm turning into toast,
But I'm too busy to even boast!

Chasing Light's Embrace

I chase the rays like a playful cat,
Dodging shadows and a hatless brat.
Sunkissed giggles escape my grin,
As bees buzz on my sticky skin.

The squirrels judge my summer plight,
While I leap and bound, what a sight!
Do I smell like flowers, oh so sweet?
Or just a bit burnt, oh well, can't beat!

Golden Embrace of Dawn

Morning's hug is a golden quilt,
Wrinkles appear, but I won't be guilt.
As laughter bursts from every pore,
I slide on grass, who needs decor?

With pancakes flying, syrup in tow,
Sunlight kisses my brow with a glow.
"Stay still!" they shout, but not today,
I twirl and leap in a sunny ballet!

Gleaming Horizons

Horizons gleam with wobbly legs,
As I attempt to do the pegs.
Slippery floors and sunbaked dreams,
Chasing moments with silly screams.

Each beam a laugh, a merry dance,
With brilliant rays that take a chance.
Oh look! A bird just stole my hat,
Now I'm the sun's own dancing brat!

Crystal Clear Glow

In the morning bright, I step on a flower,
Giggles dance with the breeze every hour.
A sunbeam lands right on my pie,
'Oh no!' I squeal, it's that hawk in the sky!

The ants disperse like they're in a race,
A slather of sunscreen all over my face.
With every drop that I fiercely defend,
I gleefully whisper, 'I'm shining, my friend!'

A Tapestry of Light

Basking in rays, I've got no chill,
Trying to sip tea, but it's spilling still.
The dog runs around with a silly bark,
While I squint bright-eyed in the noon-day park.

A butterfly lands; I stare in surprise,
Did you steal my lunch, you mischievous flies?
With laughter erupting, I happily muse,
The sun can't tell I'm wearing my 'oops' shoes!

Warmth on My Heart

As the sunbeams prance, I jump with delight,
I'm a glowing creature, a curious sight.
Trying to dance, but I trip on a roll,
Bright skin and bruises, my afternoon goal.

With ice cream in hand, I declare with a grin,
If it melts too fast, I won't know where to begin!
The laughter erupts from a dog chasing bees,
As I wave my arms, oh, please just freeze!

Touch of the Celestial

The sky shines like a disco, oh what a view,
I'm a sun-kissed muffin, and you're looking too!
A soft breeze blows, but I can't feel my hair,
It's doing flips and twirls without a care.

With a bubble in hand, I frolic and play,
While my best hat flies dramatically away.
'Catch me!' it shouts in a pirouette spin,
I beam at the sun, as the comedy begins!

Awash in Warm Afterglow

The sun kissed my cheeks, what a silly sight,
I danced with my shadow, oh what pure delight.
The rays play tag, as I run in a spree,
Next stop: a picnic, just my feet and me.

My friend, the sun, pulls out a bright chair,
A throne for my backside, it fills with hot air.
I toast like a marshmallow, slightly askew,
In this toasty adventure, I'm both old and new.

Illuminating Presence

With every inch of skin, the warmth creeps in,
Like a cat on a windowsill, grinning with sin.
I wink at a cloud, bring it back to school,
It's just not as funny when it's lost all its cool.

The squirrels laugh at me, saying I'm too loud,
But who can resist, not when sun's like a crowd?
I throw on some shades, channeling the stars,
Too bright for your eyes! Come shout from your cars.

From Dawn to Dusk

Come morning, I rise, with a squint and a grin,
    Chasing sunbeams, oh let the fun begin!
    Like a cat with a yarn, I tumble and roll,
    Sunlight, my partner, brightens the soul.

From noon's blinding spotlight, I dance like a fool,
    Thinking 'I'm cooler' as I break all the rules.
    With my silly sun hat, I spin 'til I tire,
    Even shadows join in; it's a laugh-filled choir.

A Palette of Sunshine

A painter of warmth, with colors so bold,
I brush every morning with laughter and gold.
Slathered in glow like a walking crème brûlée,
My skin's now an art piece, brightening the day.

I wear my good vibes, like a shiny new dress,
And prance through the park, oh, what a finesse!
With each ray I catch, I can't help but sing,
Beaming bright smiles, my own sunlit bling.

Splendor Beneath the Sky

Oh, how I dance with rays so bright,
Like a rooster on a thrilling flight.
My arms out wide, I start to sway,
As bees buzz by and join the fray.

In shorts so short, I strut with glee,
The neighbors laugh, they point at me!
But who can care with warmth so fine,
I'm the sun's favorite; it's my time to shine!

Skin that Glows

My skin's a canvas, bronzed and bold,
Tanned by laughter, stories told.
I'm like a buttered toast, it's true,
All golden, crispy—look at my hue!

If sun were cheese, I'd be a snack,
Melted glory, no need to act.
A walking toast, a warm delight,
Too hot to handle, but just right!

The Symphony of Brightness

The sun sings sweet, a bright allure,
Tickling my skin, I can't be sure.
Are those rays or just a prank?
My shadow dances, now it's blank!

I tiptoe on the lawn so green,
Like a baked potato, I feel so keen.
The sun's a joke, a cheeky swirl,
Laughing with me in a sunny whirl!

Flickering Moments in Gold

In patches of light, I prance around,
Like a goldfish, splashing, unbound.
With every flicker, I have my say,
Making sunbeams dance, come what may!

The shadows chase, but they are slow,
While I soak in the warmth, just so.
Funny how sunlight can be a tease,
Wrapping me tight like a warm, fuzzy breeze!

A Bright Horizon's Song

Basking like a lizard, I seem quite absurd,
With arms wide open, I become a nerd.
My shades slip down, I yell in delight,
As bees buzz by, in my sun-kissed flight.

The ice cream drips, it's melting so fast,
I chase it down, this moment should last.
Flip-flops flapping, I dance on the sand,
Like a giddy child, ice cream in hand.

Live in the Light

Why do we frown when the sun shines bright?
It tickles our skin, a reason for flight.
I trip on a ray, laughter in tow,
The grass tickles too—where did my shoe go?

I wear sunglasses, though it's just for show,
Pretending I'm cool, but oh, what a glow!
I microwave my face just to feel the heat,
And sprint to find shade—it's simply defeat!

Dappled Dreams

The sun peeks through, a playful surprise,
Each patch of light, tickling my thighs.
I spin and I hop, a clumsy ballet,
With grasshoppers chuckling, I joyfully sway.

Caught in a daze, I lay on the ground,
A blanket of warmth, such comfort I've found.
My sandwich flies by, caught up in the breeze,
I shout to the seagulls, "Just take it, please!"

Solstice Dance

In the sun's embrace, I strike a pose,
Like a disco ball, but with fewer clothes.
I wiggle and jive, a sight to be seen,
As squirrels applaud from their leafy green!

The sunburn's a badge, an emergency red,
I swear by my sunscreen, "I just want to shred!"
So grab your sun hat, don't skip the fun,
Let's laugh at the sun—oh, who needs shade run?

Gilded Whispers of Spring

Oh, the sun's a cheeky tease,
It warms my face with gentle ease.
I dance around like I'm on fire,
In grand pursuit of warmth, I aspire.

With every ray, my hair stands tall,
I swear it's trying to audition for a ball.
A hat? Oh no, can't hide this crown,
I'll bask like royalty, and wear my frown.

Sipping lemonade, feeling fine,
Like I'm on vacation, sipping wine.
My sunglasses slide down, what a sight,
A fashionista in the sunlight's light.

So here's to spring, with all its flair,
Beneath the rays, without a care.
A giggle escapes as I run about,
For in this warmth, there's no doubt!

The Dance of Light and Skin

When sunlight beams, I do a twirl,
In my backyard, I start to swirl.
A little hop, a little skip,
Tripping on air, I lose my grip.

Freckles pop like dots of fun,
Each a story under the sun.
Oh, to be a sun-kissed pie,
With crust so golden, oh me, oh my!

Staring at shadows on the grass,
I wonder if they too, can pass.
A wiggly line, a dance of light,
I might just try to take flight!

Laughter echoes, it bounces back,
As bees join in this sunny track.
A party's brewing, can't you see?
Just light, some skin, and glee for free!

Sunlit Memories

A poolside lounge, my throne, I swear,
Sunglasses on, like I don't care.
Ice cream drips and makes a mess,
'Tis the price of sun-kissed success.

With every squint, a funny face,
It's my new gig in the sunlit race.
Sunshine dances upon my nose,
A spotlight on my graceful pose.

Thoughts of beach balls, laughter rings,
And flipping toes like they have wings.
A picnic's spread, a canvas bright,
Spilling goodies, what a sight!

So let the rays tickle and play,
I'll soak the warmth, come what may.
When memories shine like the sun's golden hue,
I'll laugh at the mess—it's made just for you!

Caressing Radiance

The sunshine tickles like a cheeky friend,
On this glorious warmth, I depend.
In a sunbeam's hug, I twirl with glee,
Imagine me as a wild sunflower, free.

With arms wide, I embrace the air,
Pretending to swim, without a care.
The world is light, my worries thin,
As I soak it up, let the games begin!

Oh, look at that! A shadow race,
Chasing forms in a playful space.
I leap and bend, striking poses rare,
Like a sun god with no single care.

So here's to being silly and bold,
In the bright embrace, life unfolds.
With skin aglow and laughter's sweet song,
I'll keep dancing until the day is long!

Basking in Nature's Embrace

I lay on grass as ants march by,
A sunbeam tickles, oh my, oh my!
A squirrel scowls from up a tree,
Feeling the warmth, I'm wild and free.

With every ray, my worries flee,
A cat nearby pretends to be.
I laugh aloud, 'What a grand show!'
Nature's stage, with a sunlit glow.

The flowers giggle, swaying slow,
While bees buzz tunes in twirling flow.
I wear my shades, a stylish wink,
Sun-kissed laughter, what more to think?

So here I bask in nature's bliss,
A sunbeam dance is purest bliss.
Let warmth embrace with playful glee,
The comedy of life, just me and me.

Effervescent Light

I sprawl on loungers, drink in hand,
A sunbeam's warmth, oh it's so grand!
I feel like popcorn, ready to pop,
With every ray, I can't stop, stop!

The sun's a friend, with laughter shared,
It tickles my cheeks, who even cared?
With shadows bouncing, I play tag,
A game of light, come on, let's brag!

A seagull swoops, a feathered clown,
"Hey, what's this?" it squawks, let down!
I laugh in fits, a crazy sight,
With sunshine giggles, pure delight.

So let the bubbles rise and cheer,
This effervescent light, I hold dear.
With every chuckle, every grin,
I frolic freely, lost in spin!

Golden Embrace

Oh golden rays, you make me grin,
As I dive into this warm, soft skin.
An ice cream cone melts in my grip,
Drips down my arm, a sticky trip!

Children laugh, their shouts ring clear,
While I bask and sip a cool cold beer.
My dog joins in the sunny fun,
Chasing shadows, oh what a run!

A butterfly flits with flair and sass,
While I lay back, let life pass.
The sun's my buddy, lighting the way,
With golden love, let's play and play!

In this embrace, I'll paint my smile,
For just a moment, life's worthwhile.
With every ray, I leap and bound,
In golden laughter, pure joy found.

Warmth that Whispers

A cozy glow, a whisper soft,
It lures me out, I can't scoff!
The world's a stage, and I'm the star,
In this warm light, oh, how bizarre!

I see my shadow, what a tease,
It dances around with such great ease.
The air smells sweet, like summer pie,
With giggles trailing, I float up high.

A bee buzzes close, just wanting tea,
"Oh not for me, my drink's for me!"
I chuckle loud, the sun now smiles,
Transforming me with sunny wiles.

In this embrace, let laughter reign,
For every ray, I'll dance, no pain.
Warmth that whispers, a gentle jest,
In sunny bliss, I feel so blessed.

Sun-Kissed Reverie

Oh, the sunbeam's warm embrace,
It tickles like a playful chase.
I'm a lizard on a sunlit stone,
Wishing for snacks, all alone.

Grooving in my sun-baked bliss,
With every ray, I can't resist.
Sipping lemonade, what a treat,
Trying to dance with two left feet!

The bees buzz by, all dressed in gold,
They know where to find the bold.
Meanwhile, I just squint and grin,
As I splash sunscreen on my chin.

Oh, the funny dance of rays,
Giggling at the heat-y haze.
If sunlight were a joke, I'm hooked,
In this warm comedy, I'm booked!

Chasing Shadows in Warm Glow

Underneath the blazing sky,
My shadow plays and says hi.
It stretches out like silly strings,
And bounces back, oh what a fling!

With bare toes kissed by radiant light,
I scamper off with pure delight.
Dodging clouds like a silly fool,
Trying to keep my laughter cool.

The pavement sizzles, feels like toast,
Hey sun, you're the one I boast.
I dance in circles, feeling fine,
But trip over my own sunshine!

As daylight fades, I chase my tail,
Like a cat plotting its next fail.
In this warm embrace, I just feel free,
Who knew the sun was such a tease?

Illuminated Moments

In beams of light, I do a jig,
With arms stretched wide, I start to dig.
Dig for a snack, perhaps a pie,
Oh wait, there's just some crumbs nearby!

A beach ball bounces in the air,
I try to catch it, who would dare?
Instead it plops upon my head,
Now I wear a ball instead of bread!

I try to pose like summer's queen,
But end up looking more like a bean.
A sunhat flies away on a breeze,
At least it made some birds all sneeze!

With all this warmth, my heart runs wild,
A silly, sun-drenched, giggling child.
So if you see me laughing bright,
Know it's just me, soaking up light!

Radiance in Every Touch

In the morning glow, I start to toast,
Feeling like a buttered slice, I boast.
With every step, my shadow prances,
These sunny moments make me take chances.

Sunbeams tickle my silly nose,
As tiny ants march in a row.
They're probably gearing up for a feast,
While I'm here dancing like a beast!

With a laugh, I collapse on grass,
My energy fizzles out, alas!
But glowing up like a solar flare,
I'm convinced I'll wear this sunshine flair!

So if you see a shadowed dance,
Know it's me, lost in my trance.
For every ray that warms my day,
Brings a chuckle, come what may!

Warmth Weaved in Dreams

A sunbeam bounces off my nose,
Like a cat with its paw on my toes.
I try to waddle, but I trip and fall,
Scattering giggles, I hear them all.

With golden rays painting my cheek,
I feel like royalty, so to speak.
But as I sip lemonade, I'm dumbfounded,
My straw is missing; oh, how that astounded!

Wrapped in a blanket made of heat,
I dance like grass under tiny feet.
The sun whispers secrets, sweet and bold,
While my ice cream melts—oh, if only it were gold!

In this warm quilt where laughter blends,
I find my heart, where joy extends.
Each giggle trembles with a sunny spin,
Embracing the warmth that tickles within.

Sun-Drenched Whimsy

The sun is a jester, playing pranks,
It tickles my nose, draws giggly thanks.
I wear my shades, yet I squint with glee,
For the sun has a dance, and it's calling me!

Squirrels are bold in their nutty quest,
While I attempt to nap, who gets the rest?
With a wink and a wiggle, they leap and play,
I laugh at my dreams getting whisked away.

I strut like a peacock, feathers unfurled,
Until a sunbeam gives my hat a twirl.
I chase it down, through bushes and hay,
Only to find my own shadow at play!

A garden of giggles, blooms all around,
In this sunny realm, absurdity's found.
Laughter erupts like daisies in spring,
In the dance of the sun, I find my zing!

Lighthearted Surrender

A sunbeam whispers, 'Take a break!'
I lounge like a lizard; oh, for goodness sake!
The ants hold a meeting, and I'm the guest,
While flies stage a ballet—oh, what a fest!

I slip on my flip-flops, one goes astray,
It jumps on a beetle, and they roll away.
I laugh as the sun gives my hair a swirl,
Nothing can stop this delightful twirl!

Blinded by laughter, I try to compose,
A symphony with bees and their buzzing prose.
With lemonade dreams dripping down my chin,
I sing off-key, let this party begin!

Under the sun's spotlight, oh what a scene,
I'm the diva in chaos, bold and serene.
Wrapped in the warmth of this silly play,
I embrace the sunshine, come what may!

A Canvas of Sunbeams

I splatter my canvas with giggles and rays,
Colors of laughter fill up the days.
A paintbrush of sunlight dances with glee,
While I trip on my art—oh dear, that's just me!

Orange and yellow, my favorites by far,
I slather them on while I sing to the stars.
But oh, what's this? A rogue paint splat!
A masterpiece born from a sunny spat!

A tumble of brushes, a bright paint parade,
With shadows that shimmy, the sun won't evade.
Each chuckle a stroke of exuberant bliss,
As I slap on some green, oh! How could I miss?

Under wide skies, I craft a grand piece,
A laugh-filled mural that brings me such peace.
With sun on my skin and art quite absurd,
I live out loud, laughing without a word!

Brightness Around Me

The sun's a cheeky little brat,
Tickling me while I'm lying flat.
It teases my nose, gives my feet a glow,
And makes my ice cream melt just so!

The sky's a stage, a brilliant hue,
Where clouds play hide and seek, it's true.
I wave at them, they wave back bright,
As I roll around in pure delight!

I wear my shades, what a cool sight,
But squinting's my talent in this light.
A dance of shadows on my cheek,
A slapstick scene that's far from bleak!

Oh, warmth, you trickster, stealing my chair,
I chase you round like I'm unaware.
In this sunburnt glory, I find my place,
Laughing with joy in golden embrace.

Sun-Streaked Whispers

Sunbeams whisper secret jokes,
While I dodge sunbathers and their pokes.
A lounge chair's my throne, yes indeed,
But my bubbly drink is all I need!

The rays shine bright, all sassy and bold,
Not caring if my skin turns gold.
I chase down shadows like a silly fool,
While the ice cream truck plays its old-school tool!

I roll like a sausage in warm delight,
Poking at friends, what a funny sight!
Their laughter twirls like a kite in the air,
As I wave my arms without a care!

With a sunhat wide, I strut around,
Like a peacock who've lost its crown.
The sun's my partner in this silly dance,
We twirl and giggle, giving joy a chance!

The Sizzle of Afternoon Bliss

Oh, the afternoon sings a roasting song,
While I sizzle like bacon all day long.
With beads of sweat like jewels on my brow,
I ponder if I'm smart; I wonder how!

Flip-flops squeaking, my feet are alive,
As I strut through the park, oh, what a vibe!
The sun's frying eggs on the pavement floor,
And I'm here chuckling, wanting more!

Chasing shade like it's an Olympic sport,
I tumble and stumble, what a funny report!
Every little giggle seems to light the air,
As I pretend to cool off without a care!

The world's a griddle, I'm a pancake flip,
Sizzling and sliding, doing a little trip.
In this golden glow of a midday feast,
I bask in laughter, it never will cease!

Skin Bathed in Gold

My skin's the canvas, the sun's the brush,
Painting me silly in a radiant hush.
I look like a hot dog left on the grill,
But with each sunbeam, I get my fill!

With shades on my eyes, I'm a swaggering star,
While my hat flies off, oh, how bizarre!
I shuffle along, trying not to trip,
A spectacle happening, my comic strip!

The golden hour, oh what a tease,
Schnapping my picture as I munch on cheese.
Every laugh shared is worth its weight,
As sun-kissed strangeness becomes my fate!

So let me soak in this fiery fun,
Until evening rolls, and the daylight's done.
In this warmth, I twirl without a grin,
Skin bathed in gold, let the antics begin!

Sunlit Euphoria

When rays of gold start to tease,
I dance like I've won the lottery keys.
With shades too big and shorts so bright,
I strut around, a glorious sight.

The dog laughs, it thinks it's a game,
My legs are pale, but I don't feel shame.
Footloose and fancy, as free as a kite,
I bask in the warmth, everything feels right.

My ice cream melts faster than I can think,
The sun's so hot, it gives me a wink.
With every drip, I make a new song,
Who knew being sticky could feel so wrong?

Sun-kissed and silly, I leap with glee,
A sunburn looks great, just wait and see.
In this golden glow, I'm quite a delight,
When life gives you rays, dance into the night!

The Bliss of Open Skies

The clouds have packed up, gone on a spree,
They've left the blue for only me.
I wear my sunglasses, a fashion mishap,
But the sun's my stylist, what a cool chap!

A picnic basket filled with snacks galore,
With every bite, I just want more.
But ants have joined the feast uninvited,
Their tiny legs say, 'We're excited!'

Laughter echoes, as friends start to play,
I trip on my flip-flops, much to my dismay.
But laughter, oh laughter, it heals all the falls,
In this sunny moment, we're having a ball!

As shadows stretch and the daylight fades,
We reminisce about sweet lemonade parades.
With a goofy smile and a heart full of cheer,
I'll chase down the sun, year after year!

Warmth of a Thousand Smiles

Sunshine tickles, it knows just where,
To find the giggles hiding in my hair.
Like a warm hug from a bear with flair,
I spin around like I haven't a care.

Poolside antics and cannonballs made,
The splash is a masterpiece, I'm quite the grade.
Sunscreen mishaps lead to hilarious sights,
Who knew white noses could give such delights?

With friends taking turns, the laughter ignites,
We wear the party hats, we're in for the nights.
A toast with lemonade, a cheer quite sincere,
May the ridiculous moments bring us near.

As the stars sprinkle up in the sky,
We'll pull out our dance moves and let them fly.
The warmth we share is a treasure so rare,
With a grin so wide, I've got sunshine to spare!

Sunlight's Gentle Fingers

Those gentle fingers poke and prod,
As I flop like a fish, feeling quite odd.
In the garden, bees buzz and flirt,
While I'm here in shorts, just sprucing my dirt.

Tickled by whispers of warmth on my cheek,
I wave at the neighbors, feeling unique.
They stare and chuckle, but that's okay,
I'm living my best life in my sun-block ray.

With each passing cloud, I lift my gaze,
A playful breeze joins in with its ways.
As my hat flies off, I run in a dash,
Chasing after laughter, what a fun splash!

So here's to the tricks that the sunlight plays,
Like a goofy friend brightening up the days.
I'll soak every moment, with a grin ear to ear,
In this zany dance of warmth and cheer!

Celestial Embrace

The sun did a dance, my skin joined the beat,
In awkward steps, I shuffled my feet.
A squirrel watched close, tilted his head,
Laughing at me, it quickly fled.

The rays played tricks, a bright little tease,
I tried to strike poses, but fell to my knees.
A butterfly landed, I flashed my best grin,
But swatted it off; I forgot how to spin.

My fingers got toasty, my nose turned to toast,
As I tried to relax, but I'm laughing the most.
I called to the clouds for a little bit shade,
Instead, they just giggled and made a parade.

With each little beam, my thoughts went astray,
Might build a small fort made of sunbeams today!
But that's just too messy, it's hard to keep straight,
Who knew such fun could come from a sun-kissed fate?

The Horizon's Warm Hug

Oh look, here comes daylight, a curious sight,
It tickles my face, it's a pillow of light.
I wonder if shadows are jealous of me,
They hide from the laughter, they flee from the glee.

A sunbeam knocked twice, said, "Can I come in?"
I opened the door with a goofy, big grin.
The birds joined in, chirping tunes of delight,
While I quickly forgot how to hold still or write.

The beach called my name, said, "Come take a dip!"
But first, I fell over, and tripped on my lip.
With laughter surrounding, I sprinkled some sand,
I made a new friend, a happy sea strand!

With sunglasses crooked, I strut like a pro,
Yet managed to slip on a rogue, slimy toe.
The warmth wrapped around, a comedy show,
In this solar embrace, it's a mess of joy, though!

Prismatic Daydreams

Chasing rainbows as I doff my old hat,
Wondering if flowers know where they're at.
They're swaying in tune to the sun's silly song,
While I'm busy pondering what could go wrong.

A lizard zoomed by, said, "Did you see that?"
I nodded and laughed, while I chased after that.
My summer thoughts zigzag, a colorful blur,
As I socket some sunshine and run with the spur.

The clouds played coy, swirling with flair,
I tripped on a bubble, but who really cares?
Joined in the laughter with splashes and fun,
Letting loose under the wide-open sun.

Even the daisies don shades for a while,
They wink at the sky, all dressed in a smile.
With glittering moments in a goofy parade,
Every spark of bright joy is a memory made.

Sunlit Bliss

Woken up early by a ray in my eye,
I squawked like a chicken, oh my, oh my!
The pillow, my foe, just wouldn't let go,
So I wrestled the covers, put on quite a show.

Coffee's a-comin', just one little sip,
But the sun snatched my mug, did a flip and a dip.
I chased after it, all perky with style,
Yet tripped on the cat, wow, that's quite a mile!

With a chuckle and tumble, the world feels so bright,
Each glimmering twinkle ignites pure delight.
A pogo stick hopped in my mind for a while,
While I bounced on a beam, holding onto my smile.

As nighttime approaches with stars on the rise,
I'll sit by the moon, sharing laughter and pies.
For every sunbeam that tickled my skin,
There's joy wrapped in moments I'll always keep in.

Wanderlust Under Warmth

Oh, the sun's a sizzling frypan,
Turning my skin to a toast snack.
I dance like a chicken, I can't help it,
While my friends call, 'Give us some slack!'

With SPF as my trusty sidekick,
I prance like a lobster, oh so proud.
But when the rays get too sticky,
I hide in the shade, feeling cowed.

Every glare is a warm invitation,
To embrace the quirks of a beach bum.
I wear shades that look quite silly,
Yet I strut like a model, oh so glum!

If I could bottle this madness in cheer,
I'd sell it with giggles at the fair.
Till then, I'll bask, laugh, and shed my fear,
Embracing the chaos, the sun's warm glare.

Nature's Warm Embrace

In the park with my hat quite floppy,
I lay like a pancake, it's bliss.
Birds sing my wake-up call, quite poppy,
A picnic sans food? That's sheer abyss!

Sunscreen drips down like a slippery show,
I gaze at the sky, oh what a view!
The squirrels are plotting, don't let it go,
They think my sandwich is fair game too!

As warmth tickles toes and hair flops wild,
I laugh as my friend trips in the grass.
With every blazing beam, my heart's a child,
Chasing laughter like leaves in a mass.

But as shadows stretch, the party won't stop,
We dance like we've lost all our sense.
With nature's embrace, who needs the laptop?
In this summer dream, I'm never dense.

Daylight's Legacy

Oh, what a glorious summer fling,
My skin's a canvas, polka-dots galore!
I skip through gardens like I'm a king,
While bees think I'm their favorite chore.

Each ray's a nudge from the sun's great fork,
"More laughter, more fun, less feeling grim!"
I twirl around like a jellyfish cork,
In my sunhat that makes me look quite dim!

With every sunbeam, I channel my inner child,
I tug at my friend, "Let's race the breeze!"
As sunlight flickers, I'm still quite wild,
While ants form a line, aiming for my cheese.

As daylight fades, the stars take their turn,
But I'm still glowing with stories to share.
For every sunbeam, there's wisdom to learn,
Embracing the laughter and sun-kissed air.

Radiance in Every Breath

With a giggle, I step outside,
The sun just tickled my cheeky grin.
I'm on a quest, nowhere to hide,
With flip-flops dancing, let the fun begin!

Squirrels look jealous, plotting a scene,
While I cosplay a sun-soaked star.
My sunscreen routine's an awkward routine,
Just don't ask why I smell like a jar!

Each laugh bursts like bubbles in drinks,
Even grass stains can't dim my flair.
I relish the moment as the sunlight winks,
While friends fall over, unaware of despair.

Time's forgotten in this radiant swirl,
Every breath's a melody of light.
With silly antics, I give it a whirl,
Living my life in this sunlit delight.

Embracing the Light

I stepped outside, it's quite a scene,
My skin turned pink, like a ripe tangerine.
The neighbors stare with a puzzled look,
As I dance around like a silly crook.

Butterflies whisper, 'What's that smell?'
It's just my sunscreen—no way to tell!
I swear it's working, I won't turn brown,
Just a little crispy, like toast in town.

Birds are laughing, they think it's grand,
I'm doing the cha-cha on the sand.
With every giggle, a ray does hit,
I ponder if I'll end up fit.

So here I bask, a delightfully hot mess,
In a garden of daisies, I find my dress.
Laughter and warmth, I wear with a grin,
Who knew that sunshine could tickle within?

Luminous Lullabies

A sunbeam slides down, oh what a tease,
It kisses my nose and whispers, 'Please!'
I try to catch it, but oh, it flits,
Like a playful cat, just beyond my wits.

I think of ice cream on a summer's day,
But here I stand, baking away.
My thoughts drift to cakes and pies on display,
Yet all I get is the sun's warm sway.

The shadows giggle and dance around,
As I prance below, feet lifted from ground.
'Are you all right?' my friend queries with care,
'Just chasing the glow, I'm thriving out here!'

So let the rays play, and let them smile,
I'll twirl and I'll leap, stay here for a while.
With laughter and light, I craft my own song,
In this sunny ballet where I truly belong.

Warmth Woven in Nature

A blanket of warmth wraps me up tight,
As I dodge those ants, holding on for dear life.
The flowers nod gently, out of delight,
While I try to act graceful, but it's quite a sight.

I spill my drink, a splash and a squirt,
Laughing like crazy, covered in dirt.
Nature's my stage, and oh what a play,
With sunbeams and giggles leading the way.

Gaudy sunglasses cover my eyes,
But nothing can hide my fumbles and sighs.
As the sun spills laughter from above,
My heart dances wildly, feeling all the love.

In this sunny wonder, let's keep it light,
I'll trip over daisies, but that's all right.
With warmth all around, I swear I could sing,
Even clumsy old me can feel like a king.

Glimmers of Happiness

Oh look, a squirrel with a nut nearby,
He's nibbling away; I can't help but sigh.
As I munch my sandwich, a tiny bird swoops,
Doing tricks like it's part of a troupe.

Sunshine tickles my nose like a friend,
It whispers sweet nothings, 'Come play, let's pretend!'
I throw my worries, like confetti in air,
'Cause dancing with shadows is beyond compare.

A foot in the puddle, a splatter of glee,
Who knew being silly could set me free?
With laughter and rays lighting my way,
Every little thing turns to play on a sunny day.

So grab some ice cream, and let's be wild,
With it dribbling down, just like a child.
We'll chase bright glimmers, and laugh out loud,
In this joyous moment, we'll dance with the crowd.

Dance of the Radiant Glow

I stepped outside in my old flip-flops,
A sunbeam lands, and my laughter pops.
In a spastic jig, I twist and I twirl,
As my hat flies off, oh what a whirl!

The sunbeams play with my frosty hair,
Like a wild puppy, they tug here and there.
I swear the shadows are dancing too,
In this sunny circus, I'm the main view!

Every step's a bounce, a laughter spree,
Chasing butterflies, just my soul and me.
A squirrel mocks, with its cheeky grin,
But I am the star while the sun spins!

So let's embrace this radiant jest,
With warmth and chuckles, I am truly blessed.
As I prance and skip beneath the blue,
Who needs a stage? The world's my view!

Caressed by Daylight

In the park, where the daisies play,
The sun's a tickle, bright as a ray.
I lie down flat, arms spread wide,
Feeling like a pancake, my joy can't hide.

The sunlight giggles, oh what a tease,
It warms my nose and gives me a breeze.
With a funny hat slipping over my eyes,
I wonder if clouds ever wear funny ties!

A butterfly lands on my big toe,
We share a secret that no one will know.
As I chuckle at ants marching in line,
Under this glow, everything's fine!

The trees wave hello with a leafy cheer,
The sun's a comedian when it's near.
With every beam that winks at me,
Life's a comedy, light and carefree!

A Tapestry of Light

A tapestry woven with threads of gleam,
As I lounge outside, lost in a dream.
The sun takes a brush, paints my cheek,
Making me giggle, daring and cheeky!

Clouds drift by like cotton candy fluff,
I chase shadows, but they play rough.
Laughter erupts with a playful breeze,
"Catch me if you can!" sings the bumblebees.

With rays like ribbons, I dance in delight,
Swirling around, feeling so light.
My drinks on the table, maybe too warm,
But hey, this sun's full of charming charm!

Each beam a whisper of playful fun,
Under the watch of the laughing sun.
As I twirl and giggle, hearts will sway,
In this tapestry, let's seize the day!

The Kiss of Morning Rays

Awoken by kisses from the golden light,
I stretch like a cat, what a lovely sight!
My pajamas, wrinkled, but my spirits soar,
As I leap from my bed, calling for more!

On the balcony, sipping tea with glee,
As the sunlight tickles and dances with me.
The birds join in with their morning song,
In this good-vibes haven, I surely belong!

Neighbors squint at my unkempt hair,
But I'm just a sunflower, without a care.
The sun is my buddy, we play and laugh,
In this radiant world, we happily bask.

Every beam is a kiss, sweet and bright,
In my sunny realm, everything feels right.
With every giggle that flutters around,
Who knew morning rays could wear such a crown?

Sunlit Serenades

Oh, the sun winks down with glee,
As I stumble in my shorts, you see.
A dance of light on my bare toes,
Making friends with ants, like it knows.

I squint and squirm, it paints me red,
Like a lobster, I'll soon be fed.
Sizzling like bacon on the street,
Sunshine roasting my danceable feet.

There's laughter in each golden ray,
Who knew sunlight could have such a say?
I sing along to its glowing tune,
Waving at clouds, making them swoon.

So here I am, feeling quite bright,
Battling sunbeams, oh what a sight!
With every chuckle, every cheeky grin,
I toast to the fun that warms from within.

Basking in Golden Hues

Basking in colors, a wild parade,
I dance with shadows, so unafraid.
A sprinkle of bronzer, a splash of flair,
Who needs makeup when the sun's in the air?

I wave to squirrels, they don't wave back,
But that's their problem, I'm on the right track.
Under this sun, my worries drift,
Like a kite that flies—my spirit's gift.

Getting ready for sunbathing shenanigans,
With SPF battle, we're not enemies, friends!
One slip and slide, with a splash and a roll,
I rise like a pizza, baked in a hole.

At dusk, I'll brag about my tan,
"Check me out, I'm my own fan!"
Under this glow, I'm never alone,
With laughter and warmth—it's a sunlit zone.

When Light Meets Flesh

When warmth collides with my pale cheek,
I squeal like a pig that just found a creek.
A golden hug from the sun above,
Sending sweet beams that I can't help but love.

My fair skin blushes in the raging heat,
A comedy show, on my own two feet.
With a splash of sunscreen, I take my stand,
Dodging the neighbors with sunblock in hand.

I become a mosaic of sun and sweat,
Sticking to things, oh what a duet!
The pavement's hot, but my spirits soar,
Who knew sunshine could be such a chore?

In this radiant glow, I'll burst out in song,
With goofy moves that can't be wrong.
For every bright ray ignites my cheer,
I'll bask in delight, year after year.

Embracing the Sun's Laughter

The sun chuckles as I trip in my flip-flops,
Dodging sunbeams, never wanting it to stop.
I'm a jester in rays, with an awkward sway,
Making faces at clouds—I'm here to play.

My hat flies off while I run to the beach,
Pretending I'm cool, but I'm just out of reach.
With each step and giggle, sand clings to me,
In this sunny circus of pure glee.

It tickles my shoulders, wraps my toes,
While seagulls cackle at my fashion woes.
Strutting in shadows, like I own the scene,
In this light-hearted dance, I'm the sun's queen.

So here I shine, on this golden stage,
With all the sun's laughter, I'm filled with rage.
But not for long, I break into a spin,
For life's too absurd not to let joy win.

Sunlit Joy

Woke up one day, feeling quite bold,
Ran out the door, the warmth to behold.
Coffee spilled down, it's part of the game,
But the sun on my face makes it all seem the same.

Birds are all chirping, what a crazy sound,
They seem to be laughing, round and round.
I wave at a squirrel, he flips me the tail,
Life's a great circus, I'm riding the rail.

Sweat on my brow, it's a sticky affair,
Can't tell if I'm glowing or just in despair.
But hey, who needs cool when you shine this bright?
I'll dance in the kitchen till the fall of night.

A hat on my head, quite stylish, you see,
But the sun plays tricks, it's as crafty as me.
I duck and I dive, oh what a delight,
In the world of sunlight, everything's bright!

Bask in the Glimmer

With golden rays poking me right in the eye,
I squint like a pirate, oh me, oh my!
Slathered in lotion, it smells like a treat,
But now I'm a walking, greasy seat!

Tanning? Oh no, just trying to chill,
A noodle on the grass, what a slapstick thrill.
Lawn chair's a beast and it's flipped with a swoosh,
Now I'm just a pancake, a sun-soaked mush!

Dogs come to sniff, giving me a glare,
I giggle and wiggle, they charge like a bear.
We tumble and roll, a comical sight,
Two fools in the sun, what a wild delight!

A bug lands on me, I swat without aim,
So much for the glam, it's more like a game.
With giggles and fumbles, I bask unafraid,
In this comical dance that the sunlight displayed!

The Mirror of Daylight

Look in the mirror, who's that, oh dear?
A bronzed, goofy figure, no signs of a fear.
My hair's like a tumbleweed on a spree,
The sun's turned my scalp to a bright shade of brie!

Flipping pancakes, oh what a sight,
But the sun makes them stick; it's quite a fright.
I laugh as they flop, a breakfast ballet,
In a pancake circus, I'm center stage play!

Sweating and grinning, I take in the heat,
A towel on my head makes me look quite elite.
With shades on my nose, I strut down the lane,
Like a sun-sparkled diva, I'm dancing in rain!

Frogs croak along, they've joined in my fun,
As I slip in the grass, but oh, I still run.
With bugs on my face and a laugh that won't stop,
In the sun's bright embrace, I just can't flop!

A Glow of New Beginnings

A new day is dawning, the sky's full of cheer,
With coffee in hand, I dance with the deer.
Not really, just kidding, I'm home on my deck,
In pajamas, no less, what the heck!

Sunbeams are bouncing like kids on a spree,
I tumble through moments, oh how wild and free!
The cat thinks it's hunting me, what a grand tease,
But I'm a sunlit target, painted with ease.

Neighbors are giggling as I strut around,
In flip-flops and shades, I'm a king uncrowned.
With ice cream in hand, don't bother to glare,
I'm living my best life, with sunshine to spare!

Toasty and goofy, I'm stuck in the glow,
With crusty toast crumbs and sunshine to show.
This blissful confusion, oh what a delight,
In a world that's so silly, I shine, oh so bright!

A Symphony of Sunbeams

Oh, how the rays dance on my nose,
Tickling me gently, like a playful prose.
Each beam a sly wink, a bright little tease,
Turning my frown into giggling degrees.

The sun plays the harp, and I'm its sweet fool,
Prancing around like a whimsical tool.
Shadows are laughing, the trees nod in glee,
As I do the cha-cha with warmth around me.

Crispy skin crackles, I grin and I squint,
The weather's a bard, my sunshine is mint.
With every warm giggle, I kick up my heels,
Dancing like noodles, oh how the joy feels!

And if I should blush from this radiant glow,
I'll just blame the sun; let the good times flow!
For laughter's contagious when basking in rays,
In this goofy ballet of sunbeam displays.

Laughter in Luminescence

Under the solar spotlight, I twist and I spin,
Like a sun-drenched pancake, I skip with a grin.
The shadows start giggling, they can't help but tease,
As I trip on my flip-flops, oh, won't you please?

Melting like butter, I'm slippery and free,
Sunshine is my partner, oh what jubilee!
I wave to the clouds, they chuckle and sway,
Cheering on my cartoon-like dance of the day.

Golden confetti falls from the sky so bright,
And I catch it with laughter in pure delight.
Sipping on sunshine, my favorite kind drink,
Every smile's a bubble, propelled by the wink.

So let's bop and let's roll in this marvelous light,
Be it morning or noon, let's keep it so bright.
Chasing the rainbows like kittens we run,
In a ballet of giggles, we bask in the fun!

Caressed by Daylight

Woken by warmth, like a toaster on toast,
I bounce out of bed, oh, who could complain most?
The sun lifts my spirit with playful finesse,
Each beam a tickle, my morning's success.

I roll in the grass like a dog on a spree,
The sun is my buddy, just happy as me.
With coffee in hand and a grin on my chin,
I savor the moments, let the chuckles begin!

Birds chirp a chorus, they're laughing in flight,
While I dance in circles, quite the goofy sight.
Barefoot on the pavement, I twirl with delight,
Caressed by the glow, I'm a mess but polite!

Oh, playful sunshine, you're my favorite tease,
With every warm hug, you bring me to my knees.
I'll cartwheel through puddles, I'll dance with my cat,
In this silly parade of warmth, how about that?

Whispering Warmth

A gentle caress from the sky's golden grin,
Makes me jump like a pogo, let the silliness in!
The clouds shake their heads, I'm a sight to behold,
Pranced in the daylight like a jester of old.

With lemonade laughter and cookies galore,
I toast to the sun, oh, the fun I adore!
Shining so bright, it's a festive charade,
As my shadows do jiggles and prance in the shade.

The world is my stage, and I'm ready to shine,
Fluffing my hair, oh, what a good time!
Let the rays wrap around, like a big fluffy cat,
I'm loving this warmth; wouldn't trade it for that!

So join in the revels, under this sky so grand,
Let the sunbeam serenade lead our crazy band.
For laughter and sunlight, a comical blend,
In this merry parade, oh, where does it end?

Solace in Sunbeams

Oh, how I love it when light shines bright,
It tickles my skin, makes me take flight.
I wiggle and squirm, like a worm on a spree,
Dancing around like a leaf on a tree.

Sweaty and silly, I prance in delight,
Trying to dodge all the bugs that take flight.
A sunhat so big, I look like a fool,
But this carefree vibe? It's my golden rule.

A sunburn might come, but that's just a game,
A toast to my skin, I'll then claim my fame.
With sunscreen by day and aloe by night,
I frolic and roll, life is surely just right.

Oh, those rays keep on playing their tricks on my face,
I squint and I smile, oh, what a warm place!
With giggles and laughter, I embrace the suns' kick,
Like a cat on a windowsill, I'll just take my pick.

The Warmth That Follows

Here comes the sun with a magical tune,
I'm dancing around as it's not yet noon.
My skin sings a song of a light-hearted tale,
Like pancakes flipped high, I start to unveil.

With splashes of laughter and puddles of glee,
Getting sun-kissed feels like a grand jubilee.
I leap like a frog and then flop like a fish,
All because warmth grants me my happy wish.

The air is a blanket, not heavy but light,
While I'm out here basking till day turns to night.
I might look like bacon, all crispy and brown,
But hey, who needs shade when the fun's all around?

I'll prance like a puppy, all goofy and spry,
With rays on my face, I'll give life a try.
Silly dénouements — it's my playful quest,
To soak up the warmth, oh boy, I'm so blessed!

Kissed by the Daystar

Each beam is a nudge, a warm little poke,
As I sit here grinning, I feel like a joke.
My freckles unite, forming teams on my nose,
This radiant party, it just overflows.

With a hat made of straw, looking somewhat absurd,
I'm flipping my toes like a jolly big bird.
A splash in the pool sends the splashes my way,
Chaos and sunbeams, what a glorious day!

Oh sure, I may sizzle, but who gives a hoot?
For every odd dance makes my skin feel like fruit.
Like a peach in the sun, oh so ripe and divine,
A giggle erupts; it's the best kind of wine.

With shades that are wild and sunscreen in hand,
I'm ready for summer like a kid in a band.
So bring on the daylight and all it can send,
For laughter and warmth are the perfect blend!

Golden Threads of Bliss

Each ray is a message, a tickle, a tease,
As I shimmy and shake in the light breeze.
I'll act like a fool, it's my favorite game,
In the glow of this warmth, I can never feel lame.

With a smile that's brighter than the sun on my face,
I trip over shadows, embracing the space.
If a bird lands my head, well, that's just my luck,
Spreading my joy is the ultimate pluck.

From the morning till dusk, I frolic with glee,
The world's my parade, yes, that's how it be.
Each giggle and snicker makes my worries disperse,
As I bask in the laughter, it could not be worse!

So hand me the daylight, the fun, and the cheer,
With golden threads weaving, there's nothing to fear.
For each moment is precious, a blessing, a spin,
With sunlight as my partner, I'm ready to win!